Crossing the Wild

The 2017 Anthology of the North Cumbria Poetry Stanza
In aid of Great North Air Ambulance and Headway North Cumbria.

First published in 2017 by The Book Mill

Copyright © to the individual poems remains with the individual poets.

The rights of Kathleen Jones, Lelia Tanti, Nicola Jackson, Jacci Bulman, Kenneth Wilson, Shelagh Brown, Alison Barr, Venetia Young and Josephine Dickinson to be identified as the authors of this work has been asserted by them in accordance with the Copyright, Designs and Patents Act 1988.

All rights reserved. No part of this publication may be reproduced, stored in a retrieval system, or transmitted in any form or by any means electronic, mechanical, photocopying, recording or otherwise, without the prior permission of the copyright holder.

Book and cover design by Neil Ferber

978-0-9932045-4-8 ISBN
978-0-9932045-3-1 E-ISBN

The Book Mill
Bongate Mill, Appleby, Cumbria, CA16 6UR
www.thebookmill.co.uk
The Book Mill is an imprint of Ferber Jones ltd

North Cumbria Poetry Society Stanza

The North Cumbria Poetry Society Stanza met for its inaugural meeting in May 2015. Since then writers from across this wild and beautiful region have braved snow, floods, dark nights and long journeys to meet regularly by a log fire to read and critique each other's poetry. Meeting normally in an ancient cottage, originally the village reading room where agricultural workers would await their next day's working, the group has shared triumphs – new collections, planned readings, and news of members' travels, recommendations of journals and upcoming opportunities. The meetings have built confidence for both new and established writers. Summer 'walkabout' meetings have taken in stunning outlooks across the Pennines, and a poetry picnic beside the Raven Beck which runs into the Eden River. Much cake and coffee has been consumed.

The group now launches its first anthology. We aim to give a sense of the wide scope of poetry coming out of North Cumbria and the creative energy which this stunning landscape has always generated. We have chosen not to constrain topics to any one theme, but we hope that a real flavour of Cumbria is contained in this writing.

Our thanks to the Poetry Society and all our loyal partners and friends who have supported our endeavours in so many ways.

We will be launching the Anthology in Cumbria and also in London, courtesy of the Poetry Society who are hugely supportive of Stanza groups across the UK, see www.poetrysociety.org.uk/

We are donating all profits to our chosen charities,
Great North Air Ambulance
https://www.greatnorthairambulance.co.uk/our-services/ and Headway North Cumbria http://www.headwaynorthcumbria.org.uk/

Kathleen Jones
Lemon Tree
Wild Oats in the Olive Grove
Scorpion
How to Roast Chestnuts
The Shape of the Wind

Lelia Tanti
Heron
The Jouney Home
Spacewalk
Weathering
Garlic
Night Light

Nicola Jackson
Appleby Fair
The Ballad of Carrock Fell
Reading Rooms
Taking You to Catch the Early Train
Dear Friend

Jacci Bulman
Laid flat on the mesh-metal bridge
Where only the river flowed
Scattered atoms
Stroking my cat
5-D
You say you don't like marmalade

Kenneth Wilson
Sir Edward and His Lady
The Bed is Gone
Those Promises
Towards the End

Shelagh Brown
> Clouds
> Geese
> Cypress and Star
> The Mosque of Ibn Tulun Cairo

Alison Barr
> Nousts
> The Philosophy of Eggs
> Red Bricks and Blue Skies
> Telling the Bees
> The Screen Lass

Venetia Young
> Appleby in Winter
> Stainmore in Winter
> Still Life in a Watering Can
> The Diva Eve (Divine Productions Inc.)
> Setting Sail

Josephine Dickinson
> Earth
> Nightfall
> Elizabeth
> Oxygen

> Acknowledgements
> Poets' Biographies

Kathleen Jones

Lemon Tree

These lemons smell like
no lemons you can buy in a shop -

more lemon than lemon - sweetened
by winter cold - thick-skinned

and lumpy as toads that squat
by the cistern, under leaves of leather.

Yellow hand grenades
spitting acid.

They arrange themselves as still lives,
majolica, a fishmonger's display

suggesting pancakes, gin, a tarte citron,
the recipe for elderflower wine. Ascorbic

sucked by scurvied sailors circ-
umnavigating the world's oceans.

Wild Oats in the Olive Grove

Swinging from their straw stems like
rows of origami insects or
wild locusts, filtering the light
through pale tissue-paper wings,
spread wide to fledge a seed
stilt-legged as a crane fly, and flaunt
an underbelly furred with fine
hair to catch the wind and launch
them casually onto the breeze.

Random, reckless, extravagant
progenitors; last year's scatter
arching over the grass. The gauze
artistry of their arrangements in
pendulous, quivering imagoes.

Scorpion

A question mark on the floor
in shadow beside the shoe rack.
black patent claws
crabwise across the tiles.
I could kill it easily with
one petty crunch of my heel
this gleaming survivor
of a million holocausts -

the weaponry cocked
over its armoured carapace
like a rocket-launcher. But
I will tap my shoes carefully
every morning. Not walk
barefoot in the dark.

How To Roast Chestnuts

Split the porcupine case
and shell them from their bed of white pith
unblemished - discarding those
already bored by worm. Keep dry.
A roaring fire of wood, or charcoal.
Sprinkle salt till it turns blue
and sparks like Roman Candles.
Place the chestnuts in a cast-iron pan
with holes to encourage flames
and scorch until the skin blackens and
curls back from the wrinkled cerebellum
and they smell of ice fairs, Halloween
the street corners of a foreign town
all our northern childhoods.

The Shape of the Wind

The wind has no colour
but the things it moves;
no shape but the gaps;
a tree fallen and the rib-cage
of a roof picked bare.
The wind has no voice
but the tuning prongs of chimneys
and wires and walls and masts
singing their frequencies - their
true notes and under-notes;
a howling orchestra of silent things,
the whole sky an up-turned bell
ringing and ringing in an ocean of air.

Lelia Tanti

Heron

Angled slow deliberation and nuclear eye,
on sodden earth he walks on his reflection -
Narcissus -
stabs through his mirrored heart -
his quarry raised
to glimpse the hopeless light and vanish
in the darkness of that outstretched throat.

The Journey Home

Built with the pieces
of a half-remembered song in another language,
its words a lonely secret,
I sing it to myself sometimes, knowing
the journey home is make-believe.

Each day the end of it pushed further
as time and distance muddle what had once been clear,
the voice still cries out. When?
My journey home gets longer.

The foreign spotlight shines brightest from within
threatening to blow my cover –
I must declare myself at customs –
In the house of the dislodged,
morsels feed a habit of remembrance.
The bread I taste breaks open a familiar hunger,
delivers me once more,
to the uncharted course that will be always
the same journey home. The trail
of crumbs I left now gone, both shelter and burden
are the memories locked in my clenched fist.

Oh, if the bones of buildings
bare and naked, foundations exposed
and left to gather moss,
if only they (who know what it is to be unfinished)
could offer solace, because

the journey home will kick
like an animal in fright just
as I think I have it tamed.
Thirsty, taking more than it gives,
wanting payment
with my sleep, whispering
its half demented yearnings
in the dark –
the endless loop, the endless loop,
the crazy talk.

Space Walk

What fragile umbilical protection
against eternity's drifting -
slow dancing in amniotic fluid -
the womb ship's echoes,
its fractured voices.

So many dawns and sunsets,
life condensed, accelerated -
she could travel infinity's path -
join the meteors and space junk -
be unborn again -
above the marbled oceans of the earth,
notions seep through -
galaxies beckon -
memory's tide pulls.

Weathering

I get confused by loneliness. To whom does it belong?
Is it inherited, a melancholic heirloom
or a climatic aberration when the wind blows strong?

We have passed it to each other with a fear long
known to have us rushing from a room
that's filled with it. Loneliness, where does it belong?

Its saboteur assistants, daytime TV and alcohol, prolong
for just a while the strategy that I assume
will offer no resistance when the wind blows strong

(a hand-grenade one throws but watches land along
perimeters too close, too dangerous, too soon).
We are confused with loneliness, don't know where we belong.

I too am known to search for exits and will admit it's wrong
to have become the one for whom
denial survives as truth each time the wind blows strong.

We have watched each other's shadows far too long
to know when we have been consumed
by it. Loneliness with whom does it belong?
And will it find our hiding place when the wind blows strong?

Garlic

One. Conflict

Was it my breath drove you away?
Such otherness is often misconstrued.
I understand fear, offer no judgement.
Clanship is something I know about.
I have stood in rows all neat and obliging,
bending my head in supplication to await my turn.
Been offered to slaves, helped raise the pyramids
with promises of strength and prophylaxis –
but what promises can be delivered
under a savage sun?

And now you draw back from me repulsed.
Is it the odour seeping from my pores
makes you afraid of my corruption?
But I battled for you once against
pestilence across your lands,
while the hopelessness of it remained my loyal secret
and in dank alleys I professed to swell
love's waning passions.

Two. Ambivalent appetite

I'm worn out with the effort of reassurance.
Your constant wish to be reminded
of my potency, your need of my protection
your nocturnal fears of contamination.
Look I divide myself, I break myself in pieces for you
I dilute my powers to declare a truce.
Powdered, squeezed into vials, hung out to dry,
yet my touch alone will seep through your defences –

your resolve on moderation.
And how my kisses consume you, enter your blood ,
your soul, each breath the evidence of your desire.

Three. Courtship

Released, the redolent temptations to deliver us
not just from the insipid soup of blandness
but from the feared.
Once we were both newcomers but times change –
now the whole nation seems set to guard
against invasions of the dark unknown.

Four. Consummation

Under salt the fibres crush to yield their lure.
Caution finds no home here tonight.
We kiss only each other, secure no silver stake
is needed for the daylight hours.

Night light

Night barely skims the valley
lays its shadows fleetingly.
A transient darkness brings my bare
feet to stand on wet stone
among its remnant sounds.

In slow unveiling
it begins –
the upward tender,
the swell, the prayer
that shakes loose
from tree,
from hedgerow,
fell-side,
blackbird,
dunnock,
from the ribbon
call of curlew,
as earth anoints air
and
quite by chance,
I am blessed.

Nicola Jackson

Appleby Fair

Lean as a whippet, straight as a whip,
bareback astride with long legs trailing;
taut as the horseflesh knotted beneath you,
one hand on your hip as you twist in the saddle
to shout with an accent that cuts like a knife.

Your black mount's coat shining and plaited with water,
spawn of the wind with Spanish hauteur,
hooves strike staccato a drum beat of tarmac
cutting a swathe through the heart of the village -
a fast-trotting satyr turning your cheek.

Girls watching not looking, grizzled men line the railing
leathering tankards to toast their long travelling,
witness your moment, your time, your coming -
speed seated seamless, your hand on the pommel,
claiming your place as King of the street.

The Ballad of Carrock Fell

We clamber up the crumbling bank,
We grasp the gorse stems there,
Our feet slip on the dusty treads
While sheep gasp out for air.

Tough roots are trailing as we climb
Past tiny bluest flowers,
The flies are haloed on our heads,
Thin shadows mark the hours.

Up, up we scramble, flaiten fled,
Drag children by the hand,
Up through the gully, through the gorse,
We flee to higher land.

Up to the sheltering refuge stones
All hidden out of sight,
To wrap the childrens' dreadful cries
In folds of coldest night.

Our sentry leaned here on this rock,
He leaned on spear and spat,
He watched for rain and Romans, both
So sure to come at that.

He viewed the mounds of ancient kings
All burnished by the sky,
And eyed the gates that guard the mounds
Wherein they stately lie.

Then Romans marched there far below
And nothing could we do,
But mourn our children as we stood,
The watchers in the blue.

Around they wheeled like turning spokes,
Relentless, on they came
And climbed the gully with their Arms,
With helm and sword the same.

Our sole protection was the heights,
The rim which hid the view,
Yet up they came hand over fist;
The watchers knew they knew.

So who had told of where we hid,
Who'd let our secret out,
Was strangled by our fleeing cries
And by our childrens' shouts.

And ever on the faintest airs
Which brush the refuge stones,
You'll hear the bairdens' fading cries,
The desperate mothers' moans.

And when the gales of winter come
And grass is rimed with snow,
The keening of the winds you hear
Is asking what you know.

Reading Rooms

The way the rippled smoothing
    of the horse hair plaster feels
        the surface of ancient fingers,

touches the cut iron latch
    fashioned across the lonning
        in the village forge.

Four rooms, three children
    so they say, jostling their needs.
        So many dogs.

The way the winter sun
    lights the soft red sandstone
        almost from within.

Curved marks cut the gable wall,
    sickles sharpened by youthful hands
        or the gunnels of the rain.

The day we entered these low rooms
    and felt a coming in
        that would never leave.

Taking You to Catch the Early Train

The fells are floating, folding velvet
into deep-cut gullies where the becks
will tumble whiteness once the winter comes.
Grey cumulus wraps them with fullness,
iced with light. We cannot tell
which rim really marks the sky.

This morning my mode was London -
expecting lapsang tea, almond croissants
on the supermarket shelf. You
rattled southwards to that other life.

Now the mist is laid luscious on the land,
concealing the mighty Eden, smooth
and slow. When I cross the Bailey bridge
the waters glitter, the hippo stones
sun their backs in the transient light.

In the garden later, just the morning talk
of birds. A blue-tit nibbles the nut cage
unconcerned. The hosta stems are snapped
untidy by the encroaching season.
The lily flowers are gone from the terracotta pot
leaving the second capsule swell of seeds.

I sip fresh coffee in the punctuated silence
and wonder whether to cut them down
or no.

Dear Friend - letter from Cumbria to Grenada, January 2016

Dear friend,

Tell me about the sun.
Tell how it catches the beam ends
in your courtyard in the early
morning. Tell how
it washes pale lemons swelled
already among smooth
leaves. Help me
to remember how the warmth
filters upwards through
my jeans' skin, as we perch
to sip a welcome evening
drink, and laugh.

Tell the taste of a warm
tomato and recall for me
the fragrance of a dripping peach
peeled idle on a majolica
plate; the modest taste
of grilled fish.
Give me a hand
to believe that the air
can be other than mud,
that floods do recede
and floors dry and fishing lines
are not always used
to pull telephone lines
across the river in this modern age.

Help me to believe.

Jacci Bulman

Laid flat on the mesh-metal bridge

arms out wide,
above her a ring of silver-birch tree-tops,
the sun back-lighting their gold,
in the centre a blue autumn sky,

> strips of cirrus cloud,
> in the foreground a moth.

She thinks *nothing could be more
beautiful than this*, and knows it to be true,
in a way that clears her cells, takes away
all the clutter.

She falls asleep to the river underneath her
then wakes and the light is gone
and it is not the most beautiful
sight, is more dull, cold,

but she knows what she had seen,
and that changes the truth of everything.

Where only the river flowed

I.

He didn't know much,
only that
he needed to sleep, slept for a long time
in that room smelling of
coconut

and cheap perfume.
And she
didn't wake him.
She left the door ajar
to be sure he stayed

then let him lie there
on her cream cotton sheets
while she sat
drinking Tennessee
in the kitchen

through the hours
when even the soil is sleeping,
and then again when the
sun
was hot through the blinds.

She couldn't lie beside him,
not knowing what he'd done,
how
he'd got here
but then,

even though she knew it was wrong,
she got a kind of
ease
knowing he was
there in her bed

sleeping deeper than the well,
and for a while
she imagined
what they could have been,
the two of them

with a farm,
chickens
and a field full of barley,
way out nowhere,
where the wood axe broke the quiet.

II

He tells how she fell helping him move wood,
of the scrapes to her shins, cut knee,
how it's knocked the *zing* right out of her.

You can feel from his voice that he wishes
it was him who fell, can't quite accept how
time won't be reversed, to protect her.

Sure he knows of all the troubles going on,
beyond count, but right now his intent is pure,
there's no-one else to think about, as if

he's standing by a freezing lake and all he can see
is that one sweet coot in the lilies, limping on icy pads.

Scattered atoms

It's all about entropy:
how everything in the cosmos moves
from organised
to dispersed bits –
fancy castles becoming piles of sand.

Our love,
how does it fit with this law? My loving
your hazel eyelashes,
big smooth finger-nails,
casual left arm-swing whilst walking –

could time pick up this love,
spread it like dust in the sunlight,

so it's everywhere,
mixed with the busker's guitar-tunes in
Camden Town Underground,
the determined brush-strokes of Van Gogh?

Each ingredient: our kiss, that barking dog,
your searching hard for a line you lost –
one day all just a cocktail of murmurs
in an undifferentiated sky?

And if so, will you
draw me nearer,
draw me until the light of us,
strewn around a diluted universe
is pulled back together, collides?

Stroking my cat

Not because time may just turn up,
not because a mortal smack
has shaken every perspective –
  'make the most of this moment
  you never know when…'
not this, because the fragility
so scares me, no,
not by dueling death
but loving,
with permission to play fool with time,
to say you have no power now,
you cannot step in,
you are not the currency most precious…

5-D

I close my eyes and the aeons of past and future,
the immensity of all the universe become,
in the same moment,
like something between, (like the space
when you hold a finger and thumb intimately close together
and feel an inkling of what is possible) –
so tiny all could disappear and
so vast all boundaries lose meaning:
to escape limitation when
all that matters is that fifth dimension –
which we touch upon
when we look at someone
we can call beloved.

You say you don't like marmalade

You say you don't like marmalade
so I say it's just orange jam,

you don't like big trees
so I say they're corrals for leaves,

you think squirrels are scary,
so I say they're ponies for elves.

You say you suddenly can't spell heaven
so I say try heave (as in pull)
with an 'n' on.

You say being in this place feels weird,
so I say imagine sitting by the Mississippi
on a big log.

You say why does it all come back
the same every day,
the same world out there, in here?

I say let's close our eyes, and behind them
it can all be a perfect somewhere,

you in your cowboy clothes,
two fine grey mares standing by

while we make coffee on a campfire.
You say you don't want to close your eyes,

so I close mine, tell you of galloping horses.

Kenneth Wilson

Sir Edward and His Lady

Sir Edward and his Lady lie
Eyes' glazed gaze towards the sky.
Hand holding hand in silent sigh,
All spent they seem, and mortal dry.

Twice blessing hand held hands, St. Giles
Once saw them stand where now they lie,
Possessor's eye on brave veiled smiles,
Hard hand on stone cold hand, a child's.

Now stone in stony hand lies still,
Between the grey cathedral's aisles,
Sir Edward; while his Lady chill
Grasps *his* hand hard against his will.

The Bed is Gone

The bed is gone, the old and lumpen bed;
Gone chairs, the table new, now scarred; the man
I shared them with for fifty years is dead.

It would be better they could see some tears,
Better than dry sighs for such a span,
Such rounded, fruitful love, such fifty years.

Yes! I loved him true, with tender smother,
True to every promise hope began,
Except this guilt; I secret loved another.

Those Promises

Such vows we made to each the other,
With that wordy, weary, priest,
Signed witness by your tearful mother,
Hired suits and hotel feast!

Do you remember what we said –
The things we promised we would do –
That summer day when we were wed
On St. Giles's polished pew?

Those promises were our best prayers,
Our vows strong shorthand of intent.
Should we have known how easy layers
Are fissured, careless passions spent?

Now on my arm our daughter slow
Resolved, glides ready up that aisle;
Would I could tell her what I know,
Sad weight behind proud father's smile.

Towards the End

I'm tired; I won't walk any further.
Short bow legs of protest wobble
Like the lower lip;
Hand on stubborn hip.

The voice's small pronouncement ripples
Softly through the thinning air:
The path's too steep, too rough;
This is far enough.

Then let me hold your too-small hand
And guide you gently to the fire.
See, we're nearly there,
Nearly, nearly there.

Shelagh Brown

Clouds

In the silent night sky a crescent moon
emerges from humid, hanging clouds.
The calm sea sails on undaunted.

Sun shines on yellow wheat dotted
with radiant red poppies.
Smell of glyphosate lingers in the air.
A bright blue sky, wispy Cirrus wings.

A bank of Cumulonimbus forms,
bombs fall, flesh torn apart, witnessed by
sombre sentinels of the sky.

The clouds shed no tears at what they see...
these fires cannot be extinguished,
searching the trees for a new home,
babe clinging on.

Shots fired on the reserve,
red blood on sun dried grass,
a grotesque statue... this faceless animal.

Billows of smoke, the smudged painting
of an overcast sky
the safety blanket removed, the long death
clouded from view.

The wordless sea, the empty sky, the wheat.

Geese

Summer slipped away
darker nights arrive

in the quiet moonlit night
faint sounds of a distant

conversation
become louder
like thin ice breaking on the pond

I see them, in chevron formation,
flying across the pale full moon

from their summer by the arctic lake
among the tundra flowers,

young ones arriving for the first time
with those who have flown for years
I feel I know them well

As seasons melt into each other
they return, marking out time

I a witness to this spectacular homecoming,
from poppies burning into the crimson sky

of that last sunset
before the new moon rises
over frozen land,

and they take off into the winter whitened sky
black stitches on white cloth

in a jagged line
they pull around the cold north wind

and my heart sings.

Cypress and Star

Tall, towering citadel,
the tales that you
could tell...
Minarets and mummies,
aromatic wood burns
dark evergreen
branches
a haven
cries of Raven
silver scented
fragrance
abalm that
soothes anger
restores calm.
Cracking roots through
solid rock
you stand strong
Cyprasson's tears your sap
in mourning long
share the rivers rising mists
with grace
as the moon
admires you
in an embrace
In Vincent's last painting
you were there
an emerald obelisk,
soul laid bare.

The crescent moon
and evening star
beside you glow
two travellers on the road
would never know

In Greek mythology, Cyparissus or Kyparissos was a boy beloved by Apollo, or in some versions by other deities. In the best-known version of the story, the favourite companion of Cyparissus was a tamed stag, which he accidentally killed with his hunting javelin as it lay sleeping in the woods. The boy's grief was such that it transformed him into a cypress tree, a classical symbol of mourning. The myth is thus aetiological in explaining the relation of the tree to its cultural significance.

The Mosque of Ibn Tulun Cairo

Heat scorches clean the cobbled street
constant cacophony from the crowded souk
people packing narrow lanes,
two cats copulate in the dust.

Huge studded wooden door
Leads into cool shadow of the arcade.
We leave shoes beside the door, next to
the tidy row of plastic ship ships.

Walk, slowly through the arch
into the large bright open courtyard,
peaceful and still...
dome covered well in the centre.

A tranquil oasis in this vibrant city
feel the strong faith echoing inside
symmetrical architectural perfection
instills a sense of peace

Eyes drawn to the minaret, unique,
beautiful in its simplicity
climb the exterior spiral stairs
perfect in their imperfection.

Gaining height the wind blows strong,
breathtaking, as the views across
the city's sprawl, houses jammed
together, crowded to infinity.

'Ship ships' are flip flops.

Alison Barr

Nousts

I see them where the fields fall
to the shore in tumbles of pebbles.
A row of hollows, four yards by one,
indented, as though a giant's hand
has pressed into the earth.

Out in the timeless, sapphire Sound,
between pale Iona sands
and the pink granite of Kintra,
five boats drag sparkles of herring.
At dusk the tide carries them home.

Hands grab at coarse ropes
looped along the gunwales.
Each skiff is hauled to its noust.
Over the years keels shoogle and shift,
until the fit is snug as a glove.

I lie down in the groove,
long and bright like a herring,
long and straight like a wooden oar,
long and ribbed like a boat,
long and empty like a grave that waits.

The Philosophy of Eggs

Every morning Sinclair of Westray
placed two eggs and tea in the kettle.
He raked the ashes, set a match
to driftwood nested in the firebox.
Orange flames flickered,
chasing shadows across the room.

Pulling his jacket around broad shoulders,
he strode down the path into dawn light,
a thin line prising sky from sea.
Boots silvered with frost dust.

In the byre, flagstone floored,
fussing hens pecked at grain.
Sinclair pronged forkfuls of hay.
Lift, arc, shake, pale summer gold
shed itself through dank air,
collecting in corners and rafters.

Sweet machair straw mingled
with the sweet scent of cows
that nudged and jostled at the trough.
Outside, winter paralysed the land,
gathering ice lace around shorelines,
turning tussocks and webs to glass.

His breath steamed in the chill porch.
He hung up his old jacket,
warmed his hands at the stove.
Eggs rattled inside the kettle.
The spout beak whistled and sang.

Sinclair spooned his eggs on to the plate,
tap tapped his knife to crack the shells.
Lifting off brown stained tops,
he scooped out a bright sun in a white sky,
shiny buttercups, the colours of the gannet.

And the yolk spilling yellow at his Midas touch,
is a reminder of the other kind of yoke.
And the trust that he had in the small gleams
of treasure that the island offered,
lifted him out of the sweat and struggle.

*Sinclair was a clever man you know. His eggs
were always the best, slow cooked, just perfect.*

Red Bricks and Blue Skies

Up to their ankles in tides of red;
red dust, red clay, red bloom of effort.
My granddad and his father before him
worked at Whitehaven Brickworks.

Only Sundays could break the wall,
with a promise of fresh Solway air,
infinite blue skies and a small silver fish
caught down by the harbour on a thin line.

On Monday mornings they dragged
themselves to the temple of tall chimneys.
Grey smoke belched and gathered
above a town rendered into servitude.

Rumbling wagons tipped out rocks
to be shovelled into crusher jaws.
Millhouse wheels clattered,
screeched, ground, pressed.

Clay pudding churned in pugmills.
Hands threw clots into moulds
and packed sand-lined boxes.
Row after row, dark blood moist.

Men stacked brick upon brick
in long drying tunnels.
Air choked, powder penetrated.
Bricks smiled under pressure.

The walls of their labour rose up
around them; homes, factories,
churches, viaducts, pit buildings,
lavish Georgian houses.

Frog marks echo people and places;
Kirkhouse, Sandysike, Micklam,
Harrington, Whitehaven, Camerton,
Barrow, Romans at Brampton.

Four sided cradles and coffins
bolstered the life in-between,
decreed extrusion of the soul.
The only relief, a blue sky Sunday.

Frog Marks: These are indents in the top of the brick to be filled with mortar in order to maximise strength. Smile: A distinctive crease (smile) which appears in bricks stacked for drying and put under pressure.

Telling the Bees

He wears his Sunday best,
she a simple dress.
A gift of wedding cake
is left by the skeps,
petal-decorated.

They dance the dance of love,
bees dance the dance of flowers.

The couple set up home.
Skeps are placed in bee boles
in the south facing orchard wall.
New queens and swarms
lay claim to plaited domes.

Wax comb cells, nectar-crammed,
are fanned, transformed, capped.

A cradle is carved
to hold their son.
They tap tap the hive
with the house key
to announce his birth.

Yellow catkins, pollen loaded,
dust the swarm, honey flows.

Years pass, she passes,
it is time to talk to the bees.
Black mourning cloths
are draped over skeps.

White-cloaked hawthorns
hunched twilight ghosts.

The old man summons his son.
"When I am gone you must
tell the bees, if not they will die
and there'll be no more honey."

Mist shrouds the corpse road
from Loweswater to Saint Bees.

His son visits the hive,
tells them that father has gone.
They are the first to know.
Ice, wind, snow. Bees
murmur through stone walls.

Two guests from each farmstead
are bidden to honour Ambrose.

Hives are lifted,
carefully put back down.
The beekeeper's coffin
is lowered into the earth.
Arval ale and biscuits are offered.

Frozen silence of the grave,
warm stillness of the hive.

The Screen Lass

1

She hurries up to High Kells,
white skirts billowing.

Saltom cliffs are a red drape,
hemmed with dark seaweed,
tugged by the tide.

The horizon as thin
as a tern's wing.

She climbs down into shadows
of sea-salt and sandstone
and begins to carve.

Her initials curve
in loops of bird flight,

next to a fossil
locked in stone.

11

Now bent to her job,
she picks out slate and stone
from the coal.

After the long shift at Haig Pit
she flies along the coastal path,

runs her finger
around the smooth grooves
of her name;

bright, red, eternal.

Venetia Young

Appleby in Winter

The wintry trees shiver
and shrink into their roots,
leaving black boughs
to proudly shape the sky,
an iced blue so fragile
it seems like one warm breath
might shatter it.

Frost flowers and shells
etched on glass.
Iced grass scrunches.
makes no difference.
Glazed puddles in
slippery paths and
a smoky, warm breath.

Stainmore in Winter

All day the fell's patterns change,
as if in an evolving lithograph.
Black and white walls and crags,
scattered buildings like forgotten toys.
Brown tufts of untidy, ungrazed grass
bending, folding in the wind.
Green patches, rabbit nibbled,
roughened strips seem like
ribs in the chest of the field.
Snow fields ease into sky,
steel blue and grey.
The land shivers,
waiting for nightfall.

Still Life in a Watering Can?

Do you care if it rains and you become redundant
or maybe feel relieved of a task?
Do you look with your galvanised unicorn eye
on acres of singed grass in summer
and despair at the effort it will entail?
Do you like the sound of gumboots in gravel
Trudging around the corner
And meaning your imminent journey to your friend the garden tap?
Do you envy the hose and sprinkler teasing the children,
naked, noisy fairies shivering in droplets and rainbows?
Do you feel proud to see your watered roses
succulent and full and smelling sweet?
Do you feel resentful that sometimes
you are filled unconsenting with corroding chemicals
to shed over mossy paving stones?
Do you suffer from vanity and yearn for
your youthful complexion,
now gone and sad with rusty wrinkles?
Are you fearful that no-one will notice aging joints,
no-one will care when your handle snaps
and when your base is holed
and your incontinence splashes the unwary bare leg?
I wonder whether you will you be discarded
or retired into the role of a flower pot.

THE DIVA EVE
(Divine Productions Inc.)

God showed Eve into the garden,
where she said, 'I beg your pardon!'
when he tried to lay down all the rules.
He said; 'Now don't eat off that tree.
It will sure as sure cause dysentery.
Too much fruit will loosen up your stools.'

He said; 'Now there's the tree of knowledge
but I doubt you'll get to college.
A temptress like you won't get a PhD.'
His unfeminist critique
evoked another fit of pique
and she guzzled more fruit unashamedly.

God said; 'I'm proud of my creation,
which is divine inspiration.'
But Eve looked at God and said, 'I'm bored.'
He said: 'I'll make you a hunky boy
Brad Pitt, Achilles straight from Troy.'
'Oh no', she said. 'He's seriously flawed.'

'God, make a man with my spare parts
not ribs, not bleeding hearts nor farts.'
God said: 'Ok well what the latest rage?'
'I've got a massive haemorrhoid.'
Annoyed, God thought of Sigmund Freud
said 'No. Please let's avoid the anal stage'.

She then suggested her appendix
and her tonsils for balls and prick.
Said God: 'We need a whole man not just tackle'.
'Well how about my cellulite.
I've enough for every Israelite.'
God said: 'For my sake, cut the cackle.'

God dreamt about his story,
the power and the glory.
He hadn't even introduced the snake.
He went back to Angel Gabriel,
said: 'This film's not got a hope in hell.
Please let's start with Adam in the next take.'

Setting Sail

We have both sailed before. Sad ships were lost
and trust in journeys gone. We'll try some more.
You've said your recent life's like jetsam tossed
and mine with great relief has come ashore.

We both are skippers of our present yachts.
Can we decide who first will take the wheel?
And both let wind fill sails and hopeful hearts,
as waves hold fast the plunging depth of keel.

We're here aboard. The wind is running fair.
Cheeks glow, proud smiles as spinnaker unfurled.
Your hands and winds now ruffle my blonde hair.
The sparkling spray across the bow gets hurled.

At easy anchor now the cabin's warm.
The sailors hug. We'll weather any storm.

Josephine Dickinson

Earth

I had not before seen
such a full moon as
on the night when
shooting stars had been promised,
but instead I saw
a dog with attentive eyes,
a bright light from the house,
a river in a far off country
and heard laughter
and the rushing of water.

How was I to remake this
in the image of a woman
with a child in her arms,
with a child in her arms,
with a child in the chalice
of her smile?

after Imagen de la Tierra, from Desolación by Gabriela Mistral

Nightfall

Clouds of midges glisten
in the cooling air. Pigeons
coo, a pheasant breaks
cover, rattling and chortling.
Water chatters and bubbles
in streams and runnels near
and far. Birds paddle
their nests high up.
A rabbit dashes
across the lane. Just visible
is the line of spruce round
the edge of the field
in the deepening blue.
In a thin torch beam
sheep's eyes blaze
under the trees.
Cross Fell's blackness
rims the horizon.
Above the trees the tips
of the hills smoulder
vermilion. The grass
is cool and damp under foot.
Stars ignite in the sky.
The Plough begins its slow turn.

Back at home, I stand in the kitchen,
listening to the clock's tick
as a white light in the east
steels and grows,

this clock that will melt
in the years of silence,
melt and be replaced
by a clock said to have no tick,
a clock that travels backwards
and will stop at the moment
someone observes it,
and will start again after three days,
for no clear reason,
at the exact right time,
the dust on its rear face
sticky, intact.

Elizabeth

Elizabeth, did you see the blackbirds
fighting at dawn on the edge of the garden
as you opened the blind, turned the sheet,
smoothed the quilt, before going out
to watch William turn the topsoil
for the potatoes laid out on sacks beside him?

and did you want to lie with your head
back on the pillow dreaming, as voices
murmured in the entrance hall?

did you dream of the place where they found
the little monkey puzzle, the redwood sapling?

and did the notes of Bach's Italian Concerto
2nd Movement in d minor slowly start to spill
through the air, its turns multiplying, folding
in on themselves, fading as you moved further
into William's world and the hacking thud
of his spade spoke louder, chud, chud, chud, chud,
refreshed by the laughter of the burn?

and did the chatter of Ellen and Isabella pique
your curiosity as you pressed the heel of your hand
into hanks of warm bubbled dough, stopping now
and again to wipe the back of your hand on your brow?

did you wonder what passage Mr Shepheard
would be tasting and kneading and pulling
out before proving for the Lonsdale flock
this morning, behind his closed study door
at the top of the back staircase, where, if
she was in distress, the little Ellen would run?

what were the lights like?

and how far did you carry the coals to the fire?

the rush of water unwrapped the light,
golden at the kitchen door

did you chase the light round the house?

and did the chalk on the little blackboard
in the kitchen say

'Welcome Home'?

Oxygen

1

Water meets
soil-stuff, melting mauve,
swamp-fire, food,
two-thousand-year breath,
speaks.

2

After the tree came,
mothered in fibres
and roots and mud
and young-old worms
in the glisten left behind
after the ice,
in the marsh, the narrow
door, there too came animals
on the navigated land,
and at its feet a pebble.

3

The star holds its third child close
in water and minerals glued in the wind
against loss, for eighteen hundred million years,
in its narrow-near place, its ocean of air.

4

Star flesh becomes
roots,
water running
under the fire.

5

It is sound and voice and hearing.
It is a line
in the rushes and sedges,
a gate, a land,
for cattle,
for ark.

6

The thought of flight
burst out of the star,
a yonder place,
a mix, a purple haze,
a glugging cup,
a narrow place,
yet near.

Acknowledgements

'Taking You to Catch the Early Train' first appeared in The Way (Spring 2016) http://www.carlislediocese.org.uk/uploads/1538/the-way-spring-2016.pdf.html

'Dear Friend' first appeared in The Way (Spring 2016) http://www.carlislediocese.org.uk/uploads/1538/the-way-spring-2016.pdf.html

'Lemon Tree' and 'Scorpion' appeared in The Interpreter's House, (Spring 2015)
'The Shape of the Wind' was published in Word Bohemia (Winter 2013)
'Telling the Bees' is the title poem of the collection Telling the Bees (Words with Wings, 2015)

Who's Who – Poet Biographies

Lelia Tanti

Influences on Lelia's work derive primarily from an interest in the human experience of relationships, home, what it means to belong. Her past career as a psychotherapist leaves its unquestionable mark on her work as does the wilderness of the Pennines which have been her home for the past twenty five years.
Her work has been published by Cinnamon Press in Envoi Magazine.

Shelagh Brown

Shelagh Brown is a native Keswickian, who spent her early life among her beloved lakeland fells, reading the Lake poets, then after qualifying as a nurse/midwife, spent time in the Middle East, where she learned the art of RaqsSharqi, setting up a class for this dance back in the UK.
She became a holistic therapist, practicing Aromatherapy and Reflexology mainly. After falling in love with Egypt and its people, she met her husband out there.
Her love of poetry led her to winning the Baker prize, Moniak new writer award in 2013, and she joined local poetry groups after retirement, finally settling back in North Cumbria in 2015 where she joined the Stanza group.

Jacci Bulman

Jacci lives in a remote converted chapel in north-eastern Cumbria. She studied at Oxford University, then began to learn about healing. Jacci co-ordinates a poetry group 'The New Eden Poets' and organizes events through 'Eden 4 Poetry'. These include deep relaxation/visualisation and creative arts workshops. (eden4poetry@yahoo.com).
She has read at festivals such as 'Poetry Swindon' and will read in 2017 at Keswick WBTW literary festival. Her work is in many journals and anthologies, including 'The Poet's Quest for God' (Eyewear publishing, 2016). Her first collection 'A Whole Day Through From Waking' (Cinnamon Press, 2016) can be found at www.cinnamonpress.com or on Amazon. She has a strong faith in love.

Nicola Jackson

Nicola studied Natural Sciences at Clare College, Cambridge University, one of the first women to be admitted to the College. She took her Doctorate in behavioural neuroscience at Oxford University while spending much time on rock faces and mountain tops. She has worked in research and in community education and now writes in Cumbria and London. Her poetry is published in a number of newspapers and journals including the Morning Star and the London Progressive Journal. Her work was Commended in the 2016 Hippocrates Prize for Poetry and Medicine, and won First Prize in the 2016 National Poetry Day Message to the Planet competition. She is currently a student at Newcastle University/The Poetry School, London, taking an MA in Writing Poetry. She is the organiser of the North Cumbria Poetry Stanza group which has produced this Anthology.

Kathleen Jones

Kathleen Jones' pamphlet, *Unwritten Lives* was the winner of the Redbeck Press Prize and her first full collection, *Not Saying Goodbye at Gate 21*, published by Templar Poetry in 2011, won the Straid Award. Her second collection, *The Rainmaker's Wife*, is to be published by Indigo Dreams in 2017. A pamphlet, *The Chemical Formula of Love*, won the Iota Shots 2016 prize. She has also written two novels and eight biographies. Kathleen worked in broadcast journalism in the UK and the Middle East, taught creative writing in a number of universities, and is a Royal Literary Fund Fellow. She travels a lot and is currently living with one foot in Italy and the other in England, but hopes one day to have them both in the same country at the same time. *www.kathleenjones.co.uk*

Josephine Dickinson

Josephine Dickinson has published four collections of poetry: *Scarberry Hill* (The Rialto, 2001), *The Voice* (Flambard, 2003), *Silence Fell* (Houghton Mifflin, 2007) and *Night Journey* (Flambard, 2008). She lives on a small hill farm in Cumbria.

Photo credit: Beowulf Sheehan

Alison Barr

Alison was born in Edinburgh. She has lived and taught in Australia, Spain, and France, as well as various remote locations on the west coast of Scotland. She has now settled in the Lake District, Cumbria. Alison enjoys hiking, travelling, history, science, wildlife, cycling and strong coffee.

She has been third and highly commended in two international poetry competitions and in 2015 won the Cumbrian Literary Group poetry prize and non-fiction writing prize. Two of her poems were performed in a 'Theatre by the Lake' production. She has been published regularly in 'Northwords Now'. In November 2015 Alison was one of three winners in the Mungrisdale Poetry Competition. In March 2016 Alison was a Mirehouse 'Ways with Words' winner, as well as being long listed in the 2015 Poetry Society's 'International Poetry Competition'. She read with The Eden Poets at the 'Words by the Water' festival. Alison enjoys writing about nature, landscape and culture. This year she self-published 'Telling the Bees', a journey though Cumbria and the Celtic Fringe, and 'Memories and Moon Stones', a voyage through life. You can contact Alison and order copies at: coffeeontherocks@hotmail.co.uk,

1 copy £4, 2 copies £7, £1.30 delivery for 1, or 2.

All proceeds to Médecins Sans Frontières.

Kenneth Wilson

Kenneth Wilson lives by a lake in rural Cumbria, where he swims and plays the cello. In earlier life he founded Soul of India Tours Ltd. and City Village Ltd., a property development company. He is the author of *Orange Dust: Journeys After the Buddha*.

Venetia Young

Venetia was told at school she was a scientist and so couldn't be any good at writing. She believed this for 40 years! She became a GP and a family therapist and found that writing new stories helped some of her patients to recover from dreadful life events and so she developed the style called Narrative Therapy. She still uses stories with helping organisations to change and reinvent themselves. Since discovering the poetic form during the time of Foot and Mouth in Cumbria in 2001 in a workshop with Gerard Benson, she has written in many ways about life, love and illness. In particular recently she has discovered writing with her very elderly mother, who has moderate dementia but still retains her love of words. She has presented this work at Narrative conferences in Paris and Amsterdam. This will be the subject of a separate volume. She is a member of Lapidus, the Writing for Wellbeing Organisation. She has co-written a book called '10 minutes for the Family' with three other GP therapists. It was published by Routledge in 2004 and has recently been translated into Portuguese and Italian.

The poems she has chosen for this collection reflect her love of observing the wild outdoors and of living and being in Eden, our almost secret paradise.

www.ingramcontent.com/pod-product-compliance
Lightning Source LLC
Chambersburg PA
CBHW070548300426
44113CB00011B/1827